BY EAR

Other books by Gloria Frym:

Three Counts
Back to Forth
Impossible Affection
Second Stories: Conversations with Women Artists

BY EAR

Gloria Frym

Sun & Moon Press
Los Angeles

Book Design: Katie Messborn
Some of the works in this volume have previously appeared in *Blind Date, Exquisite Corpse, Multiples, Notus, Redstart, Shock's Bridge, The Baltimore Sun, The Taos Review, Volition,* and *Zyzzyva*.

Library of Congress Cataloging in Publication Data

Frym, Gloria
By Ear

Library of Congress
Catalog Card Number
89-085473

ISBN: 1-55713-083-3

FIRST EDITION
5 4 3 2 1

New American Poetry Series: N 6 P A

Sun & Moon Press
6148 Wilshire Boulevard
Los Angeles, California 90048

CONTENTS

III.

Reportless Subjects, to the Quick
Continual addressed—
But foreign as the Dialect
Of Danes, unto the rest.

Reportless Measures, to the Ear
Susceptive—stimulus—
But like an Oriental Tale
To others, fabulous—

—Emily Dickinson

I.

ALL OF THEM

My work comes first. They used to be my work, the days grew shorter and the silhouettes fleshed themselves out. I applaud, I shave right up to the boneline where kneecap meets the beginning of handful. So you put half the text on one side and instructions for visuals on the other. I can't get away with anything, they call my name as I step off the ferry, tanned immigrant, up to my neck in stark images. I finally got so angry I got happy and told them so, thanked them for the chance to not beat them up. I was released. The sweet melancholy of light thickening, air thinning makes me work harder. You could be my work, I could take a piece of skin and use it like a fingerprint, or the pathology of them is us. I found out about this long ago, once I imagined war, it was transparent and thus foolish, it's not evasion, it's their version. I don't care who mops the floor as long as the floor stays where it is and I wake to the trance that refreshes from the bed to the tent to the parting of the thick upper branches that have so long protected the view. Then you arrive with your amusing contours, you like my work, curiosity is the key to other, or you stay mute and there is no room for you among the merchandise. I have refused all offers thinking I have not been offered the exact amount I requested, this was my work and you were part of it. But now I admit complicity in the long line of non-elected kings, which is not blame. Your urge to collapse was also mine and my will to put my hatless face to the sun and gather freckles you already had made me. So I work as hard as I am permitted, driving by all the houses you've ever lived in.

SMOOTH ACCEPTS A STREAM

People are made out of water.
You never know who's going to stop by.
Anymore, there's no simple way to freshness.
We cast a shadow on the exposed brick.
They remember us by our profiles.

People are made.
I often lock two words together to remember one.
This area has the most complex weather in the country.
You have a lot of crazy thoughts running through your
    mind.
A complaint is a form of the ideal.

People are made out of themselves.
Hypocrisy is built into diplomacy.
Are your good friends your allies?
Belated extends the moment.
You wouldn't know that wars rage when people drive
    new cars.

People are microclimates.
Historians hallucinate history.
Many years ago there was bad blood over a piece of
    penny candy.
Relations stop nowhere.
I implore you not to peek into my closet.

People express extreme emotion over football.
It's not money, they imagine a box outside of themselves that

motivates them to work.
You can't live someone else's life for them.
One advance incubates another.
In broad daylight, I'm often afraid of the end of a line.

PHONEMIA

Still dark I could start again. When the light ascended and the birds ceased singing so much. My birds. My pride. My own public property. Confirmed by the hem of a white skirt, a braid, another century, at least, of Wisconsin. I was not in the mood for dishonesty, so I cut the words from the newspaper. Stencilling these sounds was getting me down. First, I would turn off the heat, then I would check to see if I turned off the heat. With so much to remember between waking and sleep you couldn't be sure. My sweet, sweet sparrows, where will you go when they banish the leaves. Near where the code assembles, under the wild walnut, where small animals always absorb the shock of the earth. Just around the house. I hadn't snapped my fingers in ages until they sang. Then the choir collided, clapped, collapsed. I couldn't wait for the lady, I couldn't bait the clock, each time I got there I couldn't wait to break a wing off an angel. Then I'd go home and paste it on again with a word. They were perfect now, they said nothing, nothing at all to anyone, every gesture like a chartreuse tractor lounging in a wheat field. Are you from Kansas? No, nowhere near. No casual, no cause, no alarm. I started again long before dawn, I touched my mouth to the syllable. Then I spoke.

BY EAR

One violin recalls another. The names stack horizontally, you are what you see, the aging lakes, the getting older, the getting old. Who influences you and what you do with the dangerous material you swim in, as it circles around the pronoun without reference. Optimism is my luxury, I want the fabulous excess, a picture of me and my friends in front of the brightest and most distant object made intimate by our presence. The talk is already in us, the disease there too, the work also waiting for our mouths to open wider. What is carved around the lips by disappointment, the secrets everyone else knows anyway. I read somewhere that *this* makes *that*, I didn't want to grow up, my cells took over during a partially starry night. Then my eyes began to look upon the spectacle, the birds as former dinosaurs, America, a kid without a father. We lie in store, we prepare dinner anyway or just because they say don't bother. None too soon, eyes of a widow, eyes of a child whose friend left town without saying goodbye. And the blind man says he photographs sound. Just catch the bus and make my melodies from a music box without a key. We all ignite out of an old choreography. You don't understand, to do what you do is to fight the long drawn out urge to collapse. So bring your instructions, I'll warm them up, then cross out every word.

WHO THEY WERE

The plural forms from singulars. Two makes an impossible one. Fat with itself, slower, hard to agree with. Two legs can walk down the street faster than four. If you aren't a dog.

Sometimes the closer you get to an idea, just before you have it, it contracts so that you can't even touch it though you're right next to it.

Then there's the eating of the other, communion. Becoming indistinct with the food.

What is it that one desire escalates another, and in two people, the desires are different. It's a law isn't it, that two people can't walk the same line, and if they do, one will walk off, but if they don't, one disappears.

It goes along perfectly, then it doesn't. But then it goes along perfectly.

Decay (also) turns form fluid.

She loved him well and he felt the same about her, and love had little to do with what happened to them, so this isn't a love story about two people. They had perfectly formed wills before they knew one another. Other people knew that and they were part of it. The story began long before they met, and had a way of burrowing in and rearing out at those junctures in their lives when action paused.

If the action were continuous, you could pay for the ticket, walk in, sit down and begin anywhere. You could leave saying, this is where I came in.

Another story came through, like the moment before two train cars hook up. So much of the tale began when they were separate. All of it continued through them when they were together, other stories moved in too, growing from that condition, with who they were.

You wouldn't like to see just one car on a long track, the end you couldn't see but imagine, the terrible loneliness and freedom of the singular.

(We can imagine him or her better than them.) Other opinions formed around them and were always informing them. Given the empty plain they occupy.

Till it had to come out, go somewhere, become yet another.

WHAT'S IN A NAME

Well-preserved children write off the top of their heads. A deep salmon-colored flower with a name like Gerber. I'll take you far away, while I just stick around. Isn't it time you quit leading yourself on? I heard you have everything and you're still grumbling. But what about these bugs that move across the window in sixes? Seeing their united bellies. Despots, diseases and their seasons. Your underwear just missed the basket, now calm for the first time all day. It's possible to depose a dictator in a few months, a woman did it. Incomplete sentences and you fail your boards. Give it a name, and it sounds like that forever. An essential layout sends you to the bathroom regularly. Body like a large house in which you only use one room. But what you do with what you don't use. He'd take the prize money even though he despised the donor. Words are just ideas of things. Peeling a cucumber is pleasure too. It got worse, it rained more, from more support. Instantly I saw him and started to do the same things I'd abandoned when he left. Symbols are malicious in this day. Denying the hierarchy they say they don't bow to. We wouldn't want you to think we were too happy. A man named Fox Butter? My biography, my baby pictures, my medical history—unremarkable except to my mother. Your home movies. Envelopes of ticket stubs proving that you saw, somehow.

PREPOSITION

To get past it, you have to go through it. No route around, no revolving, no light breeze. When you go through it, you wear it. If you don't go through it, you can't take it off. In the other days, in the old days, when spring was longer and summer was definite, you shined it up, you talked to it, you held it, you slept on it, but you never let it in. Reason paints a gorgeous circle around the chosen pronoun. In you, it cried to be in you, and if you ignored it, if you abandoned it, it came right back. It wants you and only you. Every long goodbye knows the preposterous wants its home. How it wants you, how you want it, how you always tell it no. You could be covered by it and then? If you were covered by it, if it were in you and surrounding you, your palms would be full of your own eyes. And could you see it then? But you could feel it, gazing at you.

MADAME BOVARY C'EST MOI

What are these words on a page, next to what is about to happen. She swallowed ink. Her legs splayed. What is this sound next to her splayed legs. She took a drink. The eyes she adored she found in books. So his aqua eyes were only eyes. And these messages promised to transcend eyes! The idea of you is as important as you.

Beat the block. Avoid the lockup. Obstruct the scattering. Draw a blank. Their faces in frame. They loved to get it wrong. And they loved us to tell. One strand of hair slipping into the butter. And the butter onto the plate in the summer, onto the tablecloth. And the slow stain. And when it would not wash, you'd remember, much later, how it got there.

Would a posy in a pot, the kind of pen I bought or not, really signify me? The bathhouse we couldn't enter, the lines you couldn't end, the one they could. The garden I took the prisoners to. Did they like it? Frolic is as frolic does across skin, money, language, crime. They leapt, they abandoned their sodas for the dark roses down the steps.

I am the golden arm of the law, the lawbreaker, the houseshaker, the dark settlement along the bank. Can you stop long enough to cross the bridge? I could also be the flounce, I have been the lowcut, the off the shoulder, the deep shadow in your eyes in the night, you remember, blinded with stars. The child who calls work by my name.

PED XING

Stop

Half the pole is in constant revolt. I don't have to tell you what the other half does. The hands of the watch are made by hands. You have to write your own jokes. Did you or would you or were. A bright shape outlined by darkness. Of course, I like trouble. Three Jews in the middle of the sidewalk, complaining and laughing. That's kids for you, they get knocked around and forget instantly and remember 30 years later. I know a woman whose passion is syntax, I know a man whose passion is passion. Soft target. I make a good sauce I live through an era with no heros. Then the movie stars take over. Why a million here, a million there, pretty soon we're talking real money. More for you. This wasn't the less I meant.

Slow

A blue moisture collects on the windows. I can't see out. A beautiful bird with a green breast could be perched in the bowers. In fact, I know the beauty is perched but I have no proof. The address that begins in me and ends in you. Was it always this way? Various African wars, the falling with no rise and the sink clogged. What do I do to make it different besides my usual. Am I allowed to cry wolf when I am wolf myself?

Men Working

We'll call you. Nothing to sell but these five potatoes and the marks I make on 500 pieces of paper. The moments that draw loopholes in time. He was looking at profit, a word I couldn't spell. Perfume lingers on my wrists, in my hair, through the seams of my shirt and it gets me a job. With a mouth like mine, I always have to shut up a little. All along I was willing it, though I didn't know that I wasn't willing. Now *yield* is the sign I find original.

THE GROVES

Long upon the cool,
the darkening waters,
a smile breaks the distance
such as the walker, the guest
among the groves most desires.

Among the groves, most desires
reverse themselves. If you are hungry
you may quench your thirst
from the dark water, a guest
of the breaking falls.

The broken distance corroborates history.
As the walker with large packages
steps aside to let a small car
cross a narrow bridge
among the groves.

So a smile is without dialect.
Most desire flutes nearer than
distant notes left on mirrors
promising more than ever
anxious futures.

Oh that the waters lighten
that the host remember the room
beneath the crumbling turret where
history corroborates the silent guest
whose fall speaks.

THE SMOLDERING BONFIRES BURST INTO FLAMES, AS USUAL

You douse it and go back to sleep. Then it arises, all around you. Oh bring me my thumb, my blanket, let me give teddy a haircut. These milk and cookies don't seem to be working, this pen is dry, this breath torn, what shall we give up next. The pretty money is burning, the ice cream is running away from us. Snails hide in the cactus, the blackberry thorny forever, spreading its roots in spite of shallow ground. We didn't know where our next concession would be coming from, but he let us see that he was close to tears. What a man! There will be no more sweeping under the floor, the former pines now moan in your kitchen. They torture the trees to make them look like gestures. So kneel before the mirror, confess yourself to yourself, you are not behind the velvet curtain, there is no stepping into the image that is you. What was the lovely excuse that sunlight provided, you found the old jewels and they were worth nothing, though they glistened in the dark with sentimental value. If you continue to wobble around in spiked heels chiquita, you will collapse the temporary staircase that leads to the stage. And she did! See, language is dangerous and he was just announcing its presence, barely its slave. I dreamed I bought a little shoe and it didn't fit, then the shoemaker came over and made me a new pair of feet. When there is something hanging in midair that I don't want to do, I feel more erotic than usual. And he got the dream of his life, when he got the girl of his dreams by refusing to dream about her anymore, though he wore a picture of her on his lapel. So much shine, building up the surface, one coat after another, far above the depth.

SPLIT INFINITE

I stumble towards a silence in order to, again, hear. The noise of monsoons. Out the back door of a perfectly American house. Still the marguerite on the step sturdily blooms. And whatever I witness comes to me through a lens shattered by the atom, different from my father's historical eyes. No science in creation, only in the thinking about it. Do we cherish or banish our deepest thought? Lessening midnight snacks, dawn's details and the past perfect. When did you say we leave for parts unknown?

The rain blew sideways across the desk. The pattern of wet on paper, a certain skid mark, several words fled down the page so that the opening phrase of the first paragraph moved down to the middle of the penultimate sentence.

I need a book of verbs. Didn't I say proceed in the voice of America and of course our bliss is part of a larger beatitude. I would have to slice the pear down the center, the impervious knife guiding my anxious pulse through another crisis. The imperfect present. You were as fractured as anyone else, though you didn't mind, then I arrived showing off my soft targets. The game of cause is rigged.

We're not simple. I told you, I've heard this sort of silence before. "To" helps the verb get through you. Then the shock of the telephone ringing for us, friends whose formal faces stay the same as ours changed. To what outside your house do you owe allegiance, beyond the obvious extensions you apply for and receive.

Staring disarms the object. I recommend this technique at all talks between hostile nations. Soft looks have been practiced by women for years.

The smoke of war disappears, the mud dries, then someone spits at the clean up crew. The state of the world interests a few people who continue to read their own minds. What would be necessary for this long walk through our new neighborhood? Resistance to the habit of mock, not carry your blue toothbrush and be late for work or not at all, then quit in the middle of a sentence. Shouldn't I know you from somewhere? Leave on the first bus.

A repertoire of facial impressions. I have a passion for abstract expressions. Hop into my adobe car. On the first day of the new year, I offered to sew a man's buttons on without political guilt.

Everyone caught in ideal Xmas all year round. Already the pictures on the table in front of the view of the tiered houses on the hill above the lake. I used to fish and now I hunt. I used to hunt and now I gather. Now I don't have to go out anymore.

We seem always to be bordering, as though time weren't running through us. A tightening of the reins and the direct assault on direction. For a while we are wrapped in the unvoiced as our protection. Now say what you love and live for it, then you'll never have to die again.

COMPLICITY

The impact of bees working together is immense. The night is discreet, though my red socks aren't and the night loves all its accomplices, the night blooms ask to be wept for, and we memorize their pungent extent and recall them when we are tired, our homes burning, and the room others offer has no floor. You were wanting something about a room, for your radiant and troubled intelligence, you had a small boy look, I was a girl there too. Then we sat down and described too much, someone's hand on our shoulders, pushing us around. Waiting for the go ahead in the long relay towards the short run. Just who is rooting for us now? The magnanimous desire trapped in you, and Spring as it orders its slow release (and every breath asks the same lovely question, Can You Imagine It?). I may never know you better than I know the intractable pronoun I circle around, but I heard you breathing terrifically fast at the top of the hill and I was breathing terrifically fast too.

ASSIGNMENT #2

Write 100 words. Cross out any you stumble on or mispronounce. Ask yourself, when you are reluctant to discard, why you need a word. You mean something, but does the word? Avoid cuteness, it dates you like a newspaper. Love me, that why I'm teaching you this. The self has artistic impulse, no matter who you are, it sculpts things to its own nature, or what affects it, paints it. In our hearts there are tiny scrolls we can never see, like the Torah, or the inside of a *mezuzah*. On them are written all that we need. Constantly take direction from this untouchable source. Yet read like you are hungry and the information gives you sustenance about lives not yours. You're beguiling when you're writing, killing the thing to make the language material. It makes you hate and worship language. Because you keep rattling the scroll house, you think you'll get in someday. But only tell a secret that retains the power of its mystery. Wear earplugs when you cross out. No sound must interfere with the sound of the text, which is, after all, your heartbeat. Flaubert reasoned with words, from his training in the law. If you don't *have* to do this, don't. Your life should depend on words, the only one worth living, though other lives remain attractive. Such as the reader's, after you've finished the work, utterly inside it and surrendered.

II.

A DAY IN THE WEST

It was 10 a.m. in Berkeley on a Tuesday.
I felt platonic
but my new grey hair wasn't doing my friends' idea of
glamour any good.
I could have eaten the sky, it was so blue that day,
no one I knew had died so why
did I study hunger instead? Cigarettes
ceased to have their meaning, drugs
out of the question, the place
I wanted so much to go back to
took on a new vagueness as though
in the middle of the night
heavy winds had torn it down. And after all, I was night
in a town with a ticket only good in the
daytime. Clearly
a long walk in a mudless park was in order.
At the Marina, leftover leftists picnicked among
dislocated workers
still loyal to the toppling buildings,
one modernist floor at a time
into the bay like clichés into the circular files
with cars we didn't need suburban lawns
we didn't want to cut anyway. In less than a decade
left hands were sewing themselves onto right arms.
I might have slipped into the finals quietly,
joined the hip flotilla on its way upstream
to aesthetic heaven.
But I bought the wrong (oh no!) bathing suit.
I said, real Italians don't even eat fresh pasta.

I wanted to start again in a sheer frock,
a heel, a black stocking, a long affair
in the darkest alley, my alley, my man
my life. I couldn't find a dark alley
anywhere in this clean clean town.

INSECT ON FLOWER

A moment of the underside, a deep yellow belly, the pause of the flicker, a small thing made large by its closeness, filling the landscape with only itself, the tone of its voice halts the weight of its meaning, what it was after was not important, what it ate was insignificant, what it wanted was not a question, trees dissemble, flowers eclipse, background evaporates, foreground dissolves into nothing but color that is about to disappear.

ELEMENTS

The creature you keep
            is shot out of sleep.
It is not gunshot
            but the hot globe
that explodes
            on its own. Sleep is short,
ammunition long. Something's
            forever deconstructing itself
and taking you with it. The
            white bird breaks its wings over you.
And you stop the bleeding
            or lose your meaning.
Jealous glass shatters
            into moments of matter.

REALISM

By January
I'm working for a company
with money.
They don't realize
they pay me
not to write
like farmers get paid
not to grow wheat. And
my music is dubious.
You would want more
than the complaints
of a commuter
in a private vehicle
along a cruel highway.
Here comes a pickup
full of Dobermans.
Parts of other trucks
fly out into my lane.
What are all those safety pins
doing on the road?
I know. I wish I had
more to offer. You would want
a story, the janitor is adorable, very
black and married to an East Indian
from Trinidad. The cafeteria
has no windows.
The woman who leases the cafeteria
posts her stepdaughter's grades
on the door

of the refrigerator.
I am afraid
of the microwave.
There is a man
who breeds birds
and eats tuna sandwiches.
There is a man
who collects Beatles'
paraphernalia.
There is a man born in Niagara Falls.
There is a woman
who wears control hose.
There is a man
who is a millionaire
who comes to work
to be like everyone else.
There is a woman
who is like a boy
who is like no one else.
There are 50 people on diets.
Three of them promise
to eat salads for lunch
and not buy Tootsie Rolls.
The characters of a place
seem bigger than life.
They are really life-size.
In the fluorescence
of the bathroom
I see an animal
who has her own fear
but never lets on.
When she flies around the room,
she pretends

she isn't out of breath
or that the bass
of someone else's music
doesn't interfere
with her own.
She wakes refreshed,
deep in song,
regardless of the gravity,
who longs for what,
how it turns out, when
the deadline.
The building
has windows that look out
but don't open. Every day
I come home and rush to
the door. A letter could be waiting
with news that I
don't have to do this
anymore.

TENANT TO LANDLORD

I rented the treetops.
I rented this window
and its relationship to the leaves.
I rented the birds.
(I must have the birds!)
I rented everything that spills
or falls around my house.
I like the spilt and the
fallen. As for the sly trombone,
he's mine. His music comes
with the rent. Music
is only second to the leaves
falling in the night
while we dream.
In the dream I always die
for the rent of beauty.
You should be paying me
living for you
as I do.

LIKE ISLANDS

The words like islands in the bay.
Swim as form of play.
The wedding night and the irrevocable.
Fortunately, I didn't have one, like that.
When they come together, what gets robbed.
But two is supposed to generate other.
Is more of the same better? This could set you free.
If the water around you weren't so cold.
If sailing were more fun than watching the regatta
from here on the hill.
You have to be grateful. Someone besides an exile
excites you. She has the accent of desire but
she can't read the word popcorn. I'm tired of cracking
the code. I had the original
in my jewelry box. But they stole it.
The refugees weren't second, though the others
acted like it, so they felt it. Ignorance
and its belligerence. Is it true that the scared are
nasty? Among cliques, you can only be friends
with who they say. Then your voice
becomes part of the water.
What a sad life he's had
even before he was born.
It wasn't always that way.
Words were more like continents.
Before thought became data.
We complain bitterly,
then we act. It takes all day
just to form one letter.

ENEMY

At least there we could see who was killing us,
falling onto the slope by a graceless bayonet,
in front of a face born thousands of years before us,
and then the cheerful clatter of metal plates passing
our way, nurses whose smiles belied the
dread, who saw the dead on their way to
heaven trying hard not to include us
in the procession too soon.

At least there we could sense a handmade knife
ready to plunge into a shoulder blade
after days of waiting, stalking the showers,
lining the yard with grinning tattoos,
warnings from eyeblinks, notes in sealed
envelopes folded to fit in the grip of a palm,
language tapped out with a spoon on a bar,
guards straining hard to decipher our code,
an old studied fear we read through the night,
fled in the morning praising the light.

But here the invisible picks us.
Folded in the masque of pleasure, riding on the limb.
Death likes his flesh. He loves to get into the blood
and let the system work for him.
Midnight throws stones
in the path of the sweet. We come home
and find the house burned down.
The preacher told the teacher
and the teacher told the town

and the town rose up
toward animal meat. It cried, hang the animal
don't let it secrete.

ALL THE MORE

I am the story of the world.
I walk around the track
with a boomerang
of my own design.

I can't hear the phone ring
as I brush my own teeth.
The call that might have changed
the color of the ceiling.

I gaze up, the foghorn calls
behind the pines.
A coat opens its lapels.
I buy a boutonniere

And scan the motherless horizon.
I slide under the marquee quickly
before my fear
of young men in small groups

Becomes obvious.
The echo of the call
that might have changed everything
joins the moan of the foghorn

And they both drift to sea
and on land the sea
disappears with the inevitable night though
I'm surrounded by both of them.

I refuse to believe
I believe secretly
and though I am trapped
I roam freely

In a kind of parole,
sentenced to relive this event
over and over
and finally remember it.

THE OPPOSITION

With no adversary. The
open invitation. The sights
reviewed again through a new
body. Nothing rushes
but rushes in your direction.
No address
but the place you pass by.
(First two rocks
that fit together, then
something an animal used to
live in.) Is the sun
tentative? No, says the morning.
Maybe, demures the afternoon. And when
the good night drapes over your wings,
two arms rest you
gently on a bed that slopes upward,
always away from you.

PLEASE

In the night
the night creatures speak.
Something unhinges the vines
and crashes into the cans.
Something in the wall sighs
from having to hold up
under hard times.
(Were they any better
when the timber had no memory?)
Something in the spring ticks
towards dawn.
On a page in a book
someone scans
the names of a man
and a woman and
an ocean or two,
the one they crossed
the one they couldn't
cross again. And then,
we have no seas, say the words,
so we have no word for sea.
And something else murmurs who,
who invited you
to the only life we try to have
without you.

THE HANDS OF THE WATCH ARE MADE BY HANDS

I'm not a surfer dragging in a shark
to make the world safe for surfing.
Whoever invented the word *time*
or any other word for that matter.
How did sounds conspire to moan.
Inside the halves, more halves always
half. Demi demi demi! The whole program
has a new cast. Comes
the memory parade of women in low cut caftans
or me recalling certain shoes
with a weepy relief that I am not pointed
in that direction today. The searchlight
casts a false heaven until
a piece of sky drops to my knees. I
secretly wish someone would push me
off the side of the pool. I keep repeating
I do know how to dive,
I do, I don't, I do.

MANIFESTO

When the yearn redoubles itself out of nothing
better to do and at midnight telegrams stop seeming
the only way to get the continuous present
to you and the rhyme sits upon the line
like the skin upon the apple and the metaphor
is the thing and the idea disappears,
the long wait for the great poem
will be over. And I'll be over in a little while
to confirm the beginning of a new poetics,
plenty of broken lines among the prosaic,
smooth lengthy generous long-legged lines,
short compact circular lines,
lines on top of lines, lines moving sideways
into each other, lines rolling all over each other,
onto the floor, all disaffection, all indifference
moved to the next line and seduced back to innocence
by a strange music whose beat
is my pulse. And I will stop insisting I know
and simply do the expert thing
which at every moment in time
is to free these lines for you.

INEXORABLE

It would always contain an element of doubt
but this was the work, and afterwards it was meant for us
to show ourselves what happens when we mix with the half
there and we are all there and getting in deeper.
And the deepest desired us, though we continued to hold out.

Now you sit underneath the light bulb that is semi-clothed
in silver so that the glare reflects upwards and the glass
of wine is lit above the stem and you are alone again
in the hard-won illumination
which is always your reward.

Who was the air of expectancy kidding,
the early fall, the long drive into the large asking.
We took pride in paying attention in ways that were
disconnected. We demanded context.
And this time
as the chronology dilated before our eyes,
the deeps predictably rising up to remind us
of what we wouldn't do just now,
we did not mind saying so in public,
imprecisely naming the gorgeousness to come. But what
about now. Would we not give in
as we remained relentless.

There was no use in telling more than you knew,
not even if you didn't know it, but I persisted
until I forgot the danger of the highest voltage
lurking, foretold, outside every house

in America, yours especially. The weapons breathed
heavily. The smoke stacks next to the
billowing flags, your country my country still
the rigid borders and the border patrol, restless and
trigger happy. So this was the liberation we spoke of
when we were given it for free? I could not have imagined
the dirty potatoes so piled next to the shiny baby grand.
I could not have imagined your emphatic desire
to pick up every grain of spilt rice from the
soft floor you paid so much to walk on.
The literalness of freedom
appalled me, you were a slave to it,
we would be nothing until we were freed from it and I
would not give in either.

Are you pedantic, do you lecture around the important,
I was once asked by a partial orphan
who had learned how not to want until forced
to want. I also would not settle for less or
take what I could like the rest of them.
I didn't come quietly to this difficult arena
and I was certain the returns would prove my present
circumstances simply a lesson, that we could,
that we could no matter what the early damages
amounted to.

Yield was the sign I found so original.
But every start resisted itself in those days.
The couch seeming more comfortable than the bed
where we once witnessed ourselves surrendering
to the dance music. No, we did not witness, we did
surrender.

But the moment we arose the ordinary miracle
disintegrated,
ideas chilled us again, we grabbed the chenille bathrobes
and headed for the living room where a
small light shed itself on a page of names. Our only
salvation.
The name was adequate to the task or it was not.
Or we were not. We ignored the telephone,
pulled the plug for if we were to answer,
the call might demand of us ourselves,
and we were tentative enough
without reminder. You were there too,
so I know you remember how even our mistakes
seemed to promise new and complicated desires
for anyone else but us.

Still we held out. All those years I wanted to disentangle
not cut but I was clumsy and short of breath, my pulse
like a rabbit stealing the night from you, so that the world
appeared my own and the headlines were enough
to make me smile ironically at the news
I had already lived through.
I do not inflate these matters, I saw the atomic mirror
and I was horrified and I kept trying not
to be though I saw your face
and you were too.

Confirmation was not enough. The need for content
was all too common, late in the age of machines
that threatened to love us to death.
Who in fact did we love
and what were we willing to do about it
and where was it written

that we should find ourselves with such voiceless clues
mixed up with remembering, failing to imagine
and that we should continue to do this so completely
that we would lose it to itself at last
and there would be each of us left to the bone,
inexorably like no one else.

There was no way of collaborating half way.
And alone you could not continue. In the morning
the night did not leave you
and in the long deconstruction that followed
a shadow imprinted itself on your face. It was not
your own shadow, it was the choice made by the dream.
And when you could not rub it off, when you could no longer
ignore it, when you were moved from the inside out,
you would be close to tears but at least
you would be close and open
to tender the only thing you ever knew
but were never ready to use,
that you would never be ready enough,
though you were curious enough, angry enough and
    softening
slowly to the strange beauty you had once called to
but could not answer.

III.

SIX OF ONE

A man I know used to joke with me frequently. About the weather, about the quality of food one could find within a certain radius of our mutual work place. Also he would stand very close to me when explaining some procedure, and he would smile in between each sentence. Often he would call my mathematical errors to my attention, though gently, with the understanding that words were my means of calculating the world, not numbers. His numbers were always accurate, and my ability to name precisely was still in apprenticeship. This man was capable of long range planning; he could foresee how many pencils a group of ten people might consume over a period of six months. I, on the other hand, was primarily concerned with what these people did with their pencils, as numbers were a kind of tyranny to me. This man might arrive in the morning as bleary eyed as I, and sensing the long and arduous night that both of us had spent separately, he with his numbers and planning and me with my words, would ask me, with a lilt in his voice, ''What do you know?'' I would generally answer, ''Not much,'' but then go on to describe some event, some headline in the morning newspaper, some billboard I had noticed on my way to work. And he, dunking a tea bag into a cup of water, would catch on to one of my phrases and almost logarithmically convert the phrase into a pun. This would always make me smile, no matter what my frame of mind. His patience seemed infinite; I began to admire him for qualities he possessed which were lacking from my own personality. This man had a nose which was similar to my father's and his coloring was also similar. Like my father, he preferred to write with blue ink, while I favored black. However, he was compassionate, which my father was not and he did not take sugar in his tea. Also he wore boots and a cowboy hat which made him appear taller than he actually was, while my father wore elevator shoes when he was courting my mother. Both men seemed to like women who talked more than they did. One night I had an erotic dream about this man; we were on the floor of the office looking for a lost paper clip. Suddenly (and much out of character), he pulled me on top of him and began to whisper numbers in my ear. In the dream I was very happy, I was a child tucked in for the night listening to a story my father was reading. Subsequently, the man ceased to look me in the eye and ever after, his sense of humor seemed strained and shy.

SUBLET

I've put all matters to do with light in the top left hand drawer. All matters of the heart are on the table, or they are sitting at the table. The silence between *at* and *home* makes all the difference, so I have put all matters of silence next to the telephone. All plant matter has been left outside, except for whatever you bring along in the cuffs of your trousers. All affairs have been filed next to the drawer containing the matters of light. If you want to review your affairs, open the drawer containing the matters of light and assemble the lantern according to the Japanese instructions translated into English. This operation is probably not necessary as you carry around with you all that matters. However, if you were in Sweden or Alaska, there would most likely be times when you would want light while all you had was darkness. (Forgive me for the slight digression, we were speaking of this house and we sincerely want you to take full advantage of it.) Care has been taken to insure your safety; should you wake in the middle of the night to the sound of choke chains clanging against the heating unit in the basement, you must go out in the rain and corner the dogs. Do not forget to grab a broomstick on your way. It will not prove an effective weapon as the dogs will merely cower in the dark and play dead. However, just curse at them loudly (so that the echo of your epithets provokes each of the neighbors in the courtyard to turn on their front porch lights in rapid succession). Then barricade the door to the basement. Later in the night, after you have settled down to dream, you may be awakened once more by a crashing sound beneath you. The dogs will dash out and you will then be able to re-barricade the door to the basement with complete confidence.

FIRST LIE

Two dolls arrived in the mail, a baby girl and a baby boy. They were dressed as infants, one in crinoline with small puffed sleeves and the other in a pair of striped shorts and a shirt with a miniature clip-on bow tie. The legs of the dolls were curled or bent like babies' legs before they learn to walk, and moveable only from the thigh. The brother and the sister liked, as many children like, to undress their dolls, to see what was underneath, to see if the dolls resembled them. In those days, boy dolls and girl dolls were made exactly the same except for the long, silky head of hair on the girl, auburn hair that grew out of roots as big as periods. One day the brother and the sister were playing in the backyard, or maybe the brother wasn't there at all, he was often not to be found, busy with one of his projects. He liked to play practical jokes. Once he removed the heads of all the sprinklers in the front yard and when the father turned on the water, the sprinkler sockets shot up great geysers. Later the brother confessed and was punished. He was always getting punished for his sloppiness and made to eat dinner alone in the breakfast nook. The brother continued to get into such small trouble that the parents spoke of sending him to military school to learn correct discipline. Two days after the dolls came, the brother had already removed the head of the boy doll and presented it to the mother just before dinner time. The day was chilly, the sister was wearing the dark blue sweater the mother had knit and she was swinging "Nancy" (as she had named the doll) by her right arm. The sister swung the doll around in a circle, around and around, twirling and twirling, becoming quite dizzy, her eyes blurring, her nose running onto her lips. The poplar trees spun, the telephone pole jumped up and down, and the rose patch where last year she dug to the other side of the world whirled in pink circles with her. Suddenly, the doll's arm snapped clear out of its socket. The sister stood in the garden, forcing the tears, with the doll's arm in her hand. The doll's body lay in the dirt, face down. The sister picked up the doll and ran to her mother, screaming, look, look what he did to my doll.

SLEEP

Sleep produces meaning. Sleep hushes the kennel. We could fall asleep sleeping, we could sleep inside a dream and dream we were asleep. Droopy around the mouth, burny around the eyes, we require sleep the bark can't wake. Sleep like smoke, like cologne, like money, undeniable. Aggressive napping. And the fall towards grace, towards what's under the ticking, towards all we can't have awake. Such as a kiss from our worst enemy, or the time he brought a new bone to our piano. There he doesn't conquer, he appears in crisp linen. The guns disappear, the snicker turns to a waterfall and we picnic among the hibiscus. Then we all fall asleep. When we wake up we yawn. Coffee sets us back. We go out shopping for nightgowns, we go downtown to buy sheets. When someone we haven't talked to in a long time phones and asks what's new, we report sleep. On a short trip to old friends, we worry. If we could only bring enough sleep. So much to sleep and so little time to do it!

OUT OF THE DREAM

A large man with a broad back announces over a loudspeaker that there will be no more dreams. Except some still can be bought as antiques or on the black market. Old dreams can be exchanged at a blues club down the street you always avoid. All those who still insist on dreams can go to one of three cities where they will find others of their kind. A lot of people will be afraid and want to stay home. They will have to make dreams in the basement which is flooded with requests and very cold this year. I ask the large man why dreams have been discontinued. He tells me that the men who make them were laid off because the men who own them decided there was not enough call for them anymore. Well, I say, what about the women. He is very silent and suddenly he falls to his knees and begins to write a confession in the mud with the tip of his index finger. Then he asks me why I don't write something too and I do and he says, gee, that's the way it should be, the lines are just regular language not poetry.

THE OPENING

At a reception, I met a man who told me his life story. Then I told him mine. All the details of each story were reduced to those elements we had in common, such as a sick mother, a disappointed father, an interest in painted chairs and old Italian neighborhoods. We talked for some time, though occasionally from the corner of my eye, other guests would wander in and out, and the glint of one brass instrument in the orchestra might make me blink. Once I noticed the light was changing around us, that a horn sounded in the distance, outside. Later I noticed that we were standing very close to one another, after he described his mother's death, and I moved away slightly. He didn't smoke, though once, towards the end of the talk, a woman approached him, put her hand in his right coat pocket and pulled out a cigarette. Immediately I turned to include her in the conversation, though I was flustered by the interruption and unsure of how to continue, as if I had been caught in a strange forbidden act.

THREE GRAPES

If you give her three grapes, she'll thank you forever. The morning after, she'll remark how lovely they are, examining their delicate stems, praising their plumpness and superior quality. These grapes are unlike any other in the whole world, she'll sigh. She'll be the one to notice how their translucent skins reveal their delicate seeds, how their colors remind her of China in springtime. Two days later she'll call long distance to tell you how sweet you were to give her those three gorgeous grapes. They're lovely, she'll wax, a month later. For a long time, when anyone stops by, she'll bring out the grapes and though they have shriveled and receded away from their former shapes, though fruit flies have found and departed the dish they occupy, she will proudly display them. Aren't they beautiful? she'll exclaim rhetorically, saving her guest the trouble of comment. In a year's time, she'll commemorate the day you gave her the three grapes and when you send her one coffee bean for her next birthday, a rapturous smile will light her face and she will praise you for giving her so many beautiful things, over the years.

DEATH & TAXES

In those days, most people were afraid to die. They were also afraid of anyone in their family dying. Dying meant that some blood relation, a spouse or a child, had to pay enormous taxes on your death. These taxes were based on your weight—a certain number of dollars per pound at death. So a skinny person would be worth less tax than a fat person. This is why some doctors advised people to slim down and why everyone became fanatic about exercise. There was no guarantee that you'd live longer if you were thinner but at least your next of kin wouldn't be liable to such a huge expenditure of capital on the event of your demise (payable within 90 days). This is why wives nagged their husbands about their expanding waistlines, why fancy restaurants served flat bowls filled with the suggestion of pasta, why anorexia became as popular as sliced bread, why people got divorced, didn't get married or lived alone, ran ads in the paper disavowing all knowledge of their husband's whereabouts, etc. If a child wanted to make a parent particularly miserable, she got fat. The State, which obviously stood to gain on every death, did all it could to keep up the death toll—airline "crashes," poisoned over-the-counter drugs, diseases transmitted through ventilation systems, food additives, minimum wages, mass cult suicide, foreign wars, heroin traffic, nuclear power "accidents," etc. Cancer and other long-term diseases were not as favored. While such maladies insured increased revenues for the State, victims often decreased in poundage so dramatically, they were worth less than the cost of the paperwork required to process their deaths.

HIGH FINANCE

The dead continue to make money. Their bankrolls do not cease just because they no longer make deposits. Their names work for them, their heirs profit by them, their reputations glow and we gladly buy their products now as much as then, if not more. In a puritan world, the dead need to work. Even they require maintenance salvation; otherwise we would forget them. Everyone works, even the unborn, as they are put to work in their mother's minds before her heart has a chance to say no. Dead authors gain piles for themselves and their neglected children. Cash has a way of exerting power in any tense or age, now or then or later. A dead waiter gets his best tips in heaven. The dead have authority in much of our negotiations. If alive they were destitute or mad, dead they accumulate revenge like interest. How else could Van Gogh, no longer a turbulent corpus, still pull the strings on the auction block? Profits continue to benefit the dead. Witness those opulent cemeteries nestled in the valley towns near Rome, crowded with monuments the size of small bungalows, where the dead live better than the living.

THE JOB

You may have the window seat. Others will want it but that is part of having it. We are giving you something nobody gets right off. We will note how you manage being new and getting the best. Others who have been here longer sit on wooden chairs. We have given you a cushioned, semi-recliner with arms. Be sure to read the instruction manual. Others will notice this combination of a window and a new chair. We know you have to sit a lot in your work here. Others will watch you watch the view of late-model cars parked in the lot. But there is also the sky, which faces south and west, and there are the pink and orange sunsets for you to enjoy. You will no doubt be here for those moments, as where else would you be? This door is alarmed, the guards come and go and freshen their smiles depending on the number of people who stay. The less people, the happier the guards. Just joking! Did you want a lamp? Notice the monarchs on their way north in the January warm front. The birds confuse them with some poisonous species and won't touch them. You can step out to see them, don't be afraid, sometimes we all step out to see them in our company tee shirts, on a balmy afternoon. We are all very nice here, we are all so compatible, we work very hard, oh that's Franz, he's been here two years, two years is a long time. The coffee is here, the toilet is over there, and then we have the machines.

NEIGHBOR

Why is she in a hurry? Why is she carrying ten books? Why is her face drawn, her eyes averted? Why was she in the driveway pushing a red wheelbarrow? What's so important to her? Why did she make her husband return the green one? Why does she bring home six sacks of groceries, they're only two people? Why is she always fixing something? Looking under the hood of her car? Why is her car always filthy? Why does she keep running over the hose? Why doesn't she use her car for weeks? Why does she always have an envelope sticking out of her purse? Why does she stand on the front steps and kiss a woman on the lips goodbye? Why does she get into cars with men she seems to know? Why does she sit on the back steps at night, under the glare of an invading moon? Why do all the children know her? Why does she laugh with them but never with us? Why is her last name different than his? Why does she drag those tiny plants, those heaps of paydirt, those 20 pound bags of 15% chicken manure up the driveway? Why does she leave her house ten times in one day and then not for days? Why do her lights sometimes burn into the dark morning and other times go out before dusk? Why is she living there? What goes on in there? Why don't we know her?

THE GUITAR HE JUST CARVED IS HANGING IN THE PLUM TREE

for Summer Brenner

You're telling me about a dream you had last night, your son is boiling a cup of soup, Cambodia is in ruins, someone's knocking on the front door, your husband is running the electric sander in the next room, the phone's ringing long distance for someone you know who lives somewhere else, in your dream the world has come to a nuclear end, your daughter is falling off the sofa, half the globe is at war, I'm blowing my nose, Frank Zappa is yodeling "My Pretty Little Jewish American Princess," what can we do about Israel, they're pulling into the driveway, it's getting harder to be poor, you're signing a receipt, the roof is leaking onto the rug, your son runs in with a splinter in his pinkie, we're rich on paper, one curtain is blowing against the stuffed monkey's tail, Anna's hummingbird is sucking at the feeder, the soup is steaming up the window, the toilet keeps flushing itself, the enchiladas are bubbling in the oven, the average Chinese worker makes $40 a month, your brother-in-law is pounding on his drums, people are still starving to death, the house is quietly slipping off its foundations, the plums are falling from the tree above the white hammock in the backyard, your braid is touching your spine, your son is calling, would you please slice the grapefruit in *quarters*, my unborn daughter is calling, please have the bed ready this time, ants are colonizing beneath our shoes, distant fires make the rising moon red, a high school girlfriend marches in with a plate of turkey breast, a child gallops through the room on a wooden horse with a mohair mane, we agree that culture is memory, knitting needles are clicking together in the next house, your husband leans against the door frame and announces, I'll be back in a few hours honey.

IN THE MUSEUM

The Titians dream they are Botticellis, the Caravaggios dream they were painted outdoors. Monet's women tire of sitting in flowerbeds and want to be Manet's girls behind pale marble counters. Junkies shoot junk in an effort to be happy. A long line of blond men march before me singing, you always wanted to be us. In the museum, I know exactly how to talk, every language is my eyes. All I have to do is replace my tongues which are moveable parts. The tongues tell me they are nipples on a baby's bottle. Everyone understands me, as though everyone were me. The paintings grow legs with feet and shoes and socks, and walk off the walls, saying, we're disgusted with all this, we want to live.

EMBODY

When the world is dark, the dreamer is busy dreaming a dream of light. Whole days drop out of the calendar while the dream moves in and makes itself comfortable. Meanwhile someone, perhaps from a military dream, is in the kitchen banging the pots and smashing the china, blue china with gold rims and tiny seahorses embossed on the undersides. The ducks on the pond are also blue, the dream is blue and filled with the smell of wet leaves. The dreamclothes of course are white, full and sexual and fresh like linen on a bed before love. Though the dream doesn't occur in a room but in a crowded city full of monuments and walls and statues of women with no arms. The dreamer is commissioned to rebuild the arms, to dive into the river and find the hands which hide under soft rocks, and to place a bracelet of moonlight and feather around each wrist. (There are plenty of blue feathers from the thoughtful blue ducks on the pond.) The dream is extremely large and covers the continents like sound. Music corresponds to the dream and the dreamer's actions, which are of course inseparable.

DIAGRAMMED SENTENCE

There, in the dream that would not end, were the same parents I had in real life. As usual, I was watching them. It wasn't a nightmare. Everyone else's parents were different. I remember thinking, you could dream any parents you wanted. I didn't want any of them. I wanted the dream to verify exactly the nature of my long observation. It was my only confirmation. The watching diagrammed its own plan.

There, in the album I used like a grammar book, was a snapshot of her in white shorts, shortly after she'd given birth to my brother. Her hair was soft brown, the sides were swept up in small pompadours, and the back was curled to her shoulders. She wore a thin blouse, tailored to the bust and she was full from afterbirth and very lovely. My father stood next to her, his head slightly cocked, leaning on her shoulder. I was not in the picture, my brother was in her arms. My father's hair was very wavy and he was fair. My mother wore an engagement ring with a large, sparkling stone that formed a small parenthesis of light above her finger. My brother's eyes were closed. None of this has ever mattered to him. I think they loved each other then.

THIN WALLS

The man who crosses the courtyard in order to get out always looks down. He speaks rapidly the few words he feels required to speak to neighbors. Since I do not appear to be old or infirm, he does not inquire about my health, but comments on the newly blossomed flowers in the garden between our houses. As he walks he slips his left hand into his pant pocket, searching for the keys he has just used to lock his door. Occasionally, when he is gone, a woman will approach his cottage. She too will look down while walking across the lawn and then disappear behind the foliage that covers the entryway to his house.

I cross the courtyard today retracing my neighbor's steps. I look down to gather clues of his path. The grass is tall enough to stay bent by footsteps. The lawn is empty except for a pair of woman's underpants resting on a twig. A small black dog darts out of the bushes followed by a large brown dog. The black dog attempts to mount the brown dog.

The man who always crosses the courtyard looking down, leaves and returns home several times a day. Each time he uses a different mode of transportation. In the morning he walks to the shed behind his house and unlocks a pale green bicycle. With his eyes averted, he wheels the bicycle across the lawn out of sight. Occasionally, he leaves home on foot. After he locks his front door, he takes his wallet out of his front pocket and removes a bus pass which he carries in his left hand as he crosses the lawn. When he gets out of his car, he never looks around.

At noon on a sunny day, a mockingbird sits on top of a telephone pole next to the house of the man who looks down. The mockingbird imitates the sounds of passing trucks. It emits a kind of giggle after each set of notes. From inside the house come kitchen sounds, plates against plates, a spoon clinking into the sink. The man opens his front door and stands on his porch holding a cast iron skillet. There is a folded omelet in the pan. The man calls out a name and the small black dog gallops up to him. The man flips the pan over and the omelet falls to the grass.

Ragweed and lambs' quarters grow against the house of the man who always looks down. Once at 3 in the morning, I was awakened by a muffled sound of glass shattering. At dawn, I was awakened again by the sound of hammering. The man across the courtyard was replacing the tiny window in his front door with a piece of yellow tin. After he finished hammering, he drew a black arrow on the tin, pointing downward.

Often the sound of a flute can be heard coming from the house of the man who looks down when he crosses the courtyard. One evening I heard the words "we're going to make you thirsty" repeated several times in rapid succession. Then I saw two quilts which bore the initials A & Z draped over the fence alongside the house. The woman who occasionally comes to visit the man when he is gone pulled the quilts off the fence. She folded them neatly, carried them across the lawn and threw them into the trash bin, her eyes focused upward.

MY ART

I clear off the desk and put a piece of paper in the typewriter. Then I remember the birthday present I forgot to send. Then the phone rings. I accept a dinner invitation for next week. Then I think about dinner two days from now. When I go to the bathroom I notice I'm out of toilet paper. So I drive to Payless and the lines are very long. Towards the back of Aisle 15A, a little boy is taking all the shampoos off the shelf. He's unscrewing the caps of each bottle and pouring the contents into a puddle. I try to find the little boy's mother or father. I go to the head of the checkstand and tell the cashier. She's arguing with a customer about his not having a current driver's license. The customer and I recognize one another but we don't know from where. Someone I spilled beer on at a baseball game last year? The cashier tells me to talk to the manager. I find the manager and I alert him to the lost little boy whose parents are still nowhere in sight. The boy has just poured the Prell green into L'Oreal yellow, it's a lovely pool, I'd like to dip my fingers in it and squish my toes in it. Instead I ask the little boy a few questions about his mother but he can't remember what she was wearing. The manager asks if I'll accompany the little boy to the police station. I say okay, the little boy is crying, and on the way over I try to tell him a story.

PERFECT

A small stocky German, his large Mexican wife, and their several children of various shades of brown sit under a *palapa* at a seaside resort. The children, all but the youngest, suddenly run off to the shore's edge to look for shells. The man lifts his eyes from a book and his gaze follows the children into a wave. He is here to avoid the insistent drive of his own kind for perfection. He forsakes the stridencies of his native language for the sonorous melodies of Spanish. Unkempt vacationers, seaweed mixed with smashed plastic cups along a beach recently ravaged by hurricane, flies diving into the watermelon on the driftwood table before him, street smells of garlic, refuse and diesel, the perpetual construction and deconstruction of the hotel—bricks and tiles loosened and ready to fall after only a year or two since their placement, curtains hanging askew from rods whose fixtures pull away from the plaster soon after the carpenters have left—all of this enters him and pleases him. He looks at his wife's small, fleshy hands holding a book by a popular North American author, their youngest child contentedly transferring sand from the beach into her pink, plastic shoes, a large nautical hat keeping the noon sun from her pale face. A dark boy passes by with a tray of mangoes on sticks, peeled, cut and glistening. The boy approaches the man and the man asks, *cuanto cuestan*? An exchange of pesos is made and the man hands the mango to his youngest daughter. The girl bites into the fruit and juice runs down her chin. She giggles. Before she is finished, another vendor floats up to the family with helium balloons on strings. The man buys a balloon with kittens on it and ties the string to his daughter's wrist. She is overtaken with glee, glee in fact issues from her small squeals and bobbing eyes. The man sits back and admires his daughter's happiness. Occasionally the wife looks up from her book with a soft, indulgent smile. The thatch of the palapa stirs in the salty breeze. Small but visible tears begin to roll down the German's face. The breeze thickens into a wind that carries the tears to sea. It is hopeless, the man thinks, hopeless. It is all so perfect.

CHAPTERS FOR YOU

I was just finishing a tangerine, the peels curled on the table next to your knees, the seeds were still cupped in my palms, the veranda was fragrant with the faint of citrus, no one else was in the air we were breathing, except everyone was. Two books lay open flat, their spines almost cracking, we sat among the scattered letters, I read you a chapter of the most beautiful book on earth, we outlined the vista, we stepped out, a taxi pulled up to our feet, a coconut fell to our ankles, a shrimp swam into our hands, a palm frond brushed against our shoulders, at night a small animal spoke to us in a secret language, the water broke closer and closer to shore, a child told us a pleasant history of the world, a horse cantered by to entertain us, five dogs and five boys walked the beach abreast swinging iguanas by their tails, someone held out his hand to ask for something we always had but could never give before, a catamaran hailed us, our country left us as the flags of everywhere waved us on, the waves were warm and desired our shoulders, the sun was hot and wanted nothing more than to make us it, all the news the paperboys sold was old, the real news was the footprints our feet made in the sand, we walked very close, we dipped ourselves in the element we were born to, we talked very close, a word passed from my lips to yours and didn't burn, we didn't smile readily though we laughed plenty, we ordered nothing, the waiters read our minds and brought us beers made from waters deeper than we knew, we brushed the sand from our toes, we took off our clothes, revealed our pale undersides, our browning thighs, our well- defined calves, and a small crowd of bathers gathered against the blue and the white, against the table of the shore and the lip of the sea, and applauded us in our important abandon.